Conquering
Kindergarten

Reading
Mathematics
Science
Social Studies
Writing

Jodene Lynn Smith, M.A.

Publishing Credits

Corinne Burton, M.A.Ed., *President*; Conni Medina, M.A.Ed., *Managing Editor*; Emily R. Smith, M.A.Ed., *Content Director*; Lynette Ordoñez, *Editor*; Evan Ferrell, *Graphic Designer*; Lubabah Memon, *Assistant Editor*

Image Credits

pp. 82, 112, 127, 142 Illustrations by Maple Lam; all other images from iStock and/or Shutterstock.

Standards

Shell Education
A division of Teacher Created Materials
5301 Oceanus Drive
Huntington Beach, CA 92649-1030

www.tcmpub.com/shell-education
ISBN 978-1-4258-1619-3
©2017 Shell Education Publishing, Inc.

Table of Contents

Dear Family,

Welcome to *Conquering Kindergarten*. Kindergarten will be an exciting and challenging year for your child. This book is designed to supplement the concepts your child is learning in kindergarten and to strengthen the connection between home and school. The activities in this book are based on today's standards and will help your child develop essential skills in reading, word study, language, writing, mathematics, social studies, and science. It also features fun, yet challenging, critical-thinking activities and games. In addition to the activity sheets in this book, the end of each section also provides engaging extension activities.

Your child should complete one unit per month, including the extension activities. This will allow your child to think about grade-level concepts over a longer period of time. This also ensures that the book can be completed in one school year. Since your child is developing his or her skills, it is important that you work through the activities in this book with him or her.

Keep these tips in mind as you work with your child this year:

- Set aside specific times each week to work on the activities.

- Have your child complete one or two activities each time, rather than an entire unit at one time.

- Keep all practice sessions with your child positive and constructive. If the mood becomes tense or you and your child get frustrated, set the book aside and find another time to practice.

- Read the directions aloud to your child. If your child is having difficulty understanding what to do, work through some of the problems together.

- Play the games with your child. Read the directions and explain the rules to your child. Then, have fun playing and learning together.

- Encourage your child to do his or her best work, and compliment the effort that goes into learning.

Enjoy the time learning with your child during kindergarten. Summer will be here before you know it!

Sincerely,

The Shell Education Staff

Suggested Family Activities

You can extend your child's learning by taking fun family field trips. A wide variety of experiences helps expand and develop a child's vocabulary. Field trips also provide greater context and meaning to his or her learning in school.

A Trip to a Zoo

Before your trip, create a Zoo Bingo card. Include pictures of a variety of animals you will see at the zoo. Bring the Zoo Bingo card with you. As you spend the day exploring, have your child cross out each animal you come across. When he or she gets bingo, celebrate the accomplishment!

A Trip to a Museum

Play a family game in the museum. Have your child pick an artifact, piece of art, etc., without telling the other players what it is. The other players then try to guess what the secret item is. Ask for clues that require a yes or no answer. For example, "Does the item have sharp teeth?," or "Is the item made out of clay?" The person who guesses the secret item correctly gets to choose the item in the next room.

A Trip to a Library

Have your child pick books he or she has never read (or that you have never read to him or her). Look carefully at the covers of the books together. Ask your child what he or she thinks the stories are going to be about based on the covers alone. Then, read the books aloud to your child, and see if his or her guess was correct.

A Trip to a National Park

The National Park Service has a great program called Junior Rangers. If you go to a local park, check in with the rangers at the visitors center to see what tasks your child can complete to earn a Junior Ranger patch and/or certificate. Your child can also go to the WebRangers site (www.nps.gov/webrangers/) and check out a vacation spot, play games, and earn virtual rewards!

A Trip to a Monument or Memorial

Ahead of time, look up some interesting stories about the person who is honored by the monument/memorial. Focus on stories about the person's childhood or early accomplishments, as those will be more relatable to your child. As you stand and look at the monument/memorial, tell the stories and ask your child to describe what kind of monument/memorial he or she thinks could be built for him or her someday!

Suggested Family Activities (cont.)

By discussing the activities in this book, you can enhance your child's learning. But it doesn't have to stop there. The suggestions below provide even more ideas on how to support your child's education.

General Skills

- Make sure your child gets plenty of sleep. Children this age need between 9–11 hours of sleep each night. Establish a nightly bedtime routine that involves relaxing activities, such as a warm shower or bath or reading a story.

- Help your child become organized and responsible by setting a good example. Have places to keep important things. Make to-do lists of your chores or errands. When your child sees you making time for those things, he or she will recognize that organization and responsibility are important.

Reading Skills

- Create an alphabet book with your child. Go through old magazines, newspapers, advertisements, etc., to find an image for each letter of the alphabet. Help your child cut out the images and glue them into a book.

- Set a reading time for the entire family at least every other day. Have your child read familiar words or letters. Point to words that he or she may already know (or words that are similar to ones he or she already knows), and have your child sound them out.

Writing Skills

- Have your child practice writing letters through sensory activities. For example, you could pour an impressionable substance (this could be salt, flour, sugar, pudding, shaving cream, etc.) into a cookie tray and let your child get messy while learning to write letters.

- Supply your child with writing tools that better fit his or her hands to help develop his or her fine motor skills. Normal-length pencils are often too large and are awkward for smaller hands to hold. Golf pencils, broken crayons, and small markers will make writing more comfortable.

Mathematics Skills

- Help your child practice counting, whenever possible. You can do this in everyday situations such as counting the number of stairs, silverware pieces at the dinner table, etc.

- Involve your child in grocery shopping. Ask him or her to help solve basic mathematical problems. For example, "I have two apples in my hands. You have two apples in yours. How many apples do we have altogether?"

Directions: Match the words to the pictures.

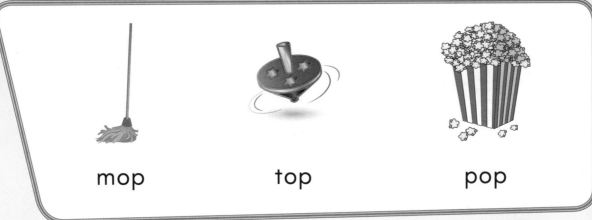

mop   top   pop

1 top

2 mop

3 pop

Directions: Circle the word for the picture. Write the word.

4

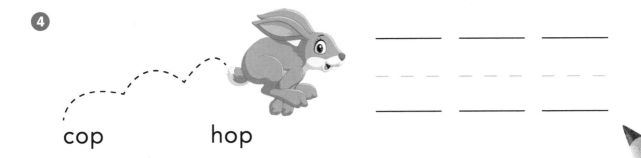

cop   hop

_____ _____ _____

_ _ _ _ _ _ _ _ _ _ _ _

_____ _____ _____

Directions: Match the words to the pictures.

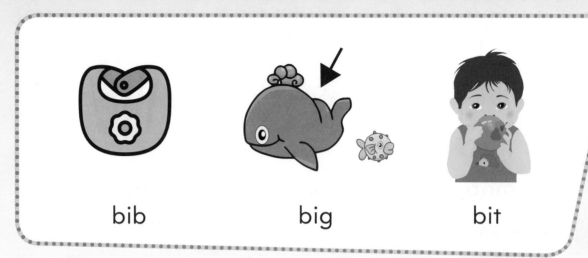

bib   big   bit

1 big

2 bib

3 bit

Directions: Circle the word for the picture. Write the word.

4

bin   bid

_____ _____ _____

- - - - - - - - - - - - - -

_____ _____ _____

Directions: Read each word. Draw lines between the matching words.

the

of

and

a

to

of

the

and

to

a

Language

Directions: Draw lines to match the pictures to the prepositions.

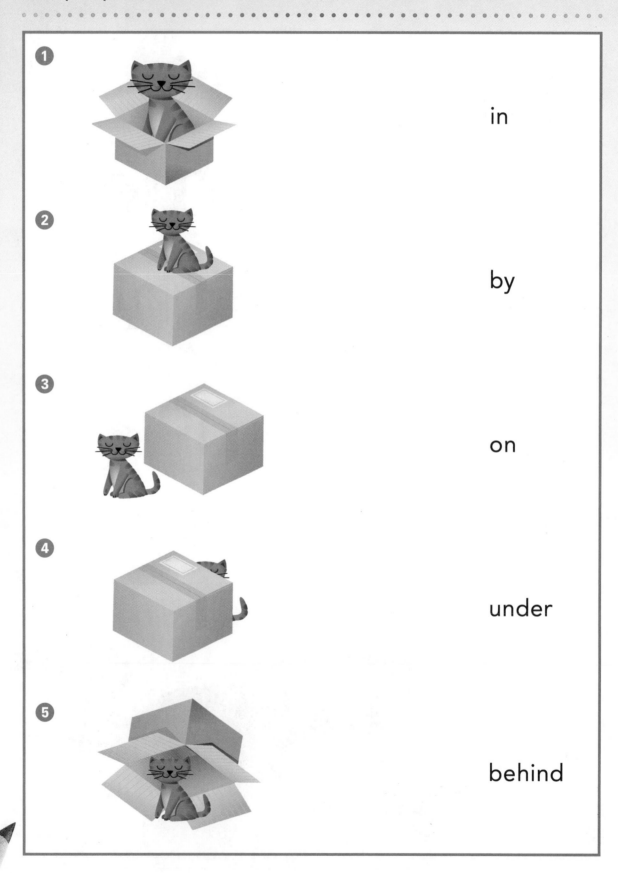

1   in

2   by

3   on

4   under

5   behind

Directions: Think about a picnic at the park. Draw notes about the day.

Who?

Where?

When?

Event 1

Event 2

Directions: Write about a picnic. Fill in the checklist.

Introduction

_____

I had a picnic with _____ .

Events

_____

First, _____ .

Then, _____ .

Closing Sentence

_____

_____ ,

and I had so much fun!

☑ Checklist

☐ I have an introduction.

☐ I have events.

☐ I have a closing.

Directions: Solve each problem.

1 Count how many stars in all.

_____

_ _ _ _ _ _

_____

4 Count how many animals in all.

_____

_ _ _ _ _ _

_____

2 Count how many hearts in all.

_____

_ _ _ _ _ _

_____

5 Count how many books in all.

_____

_ _ _ _ _ _

_____

3 Count how many cookies in all.

_____

_____

6 Count how many turtles in all.

_____

_____

Directions: Circle the answer.

1 Will every bunny get a carrot?

yes   no

2 Will every boy get a cap?

yes   no

3 Will every dog get a bone?

yes   no

4 Will every cupcake get a cherry?

yes   no

Directions: Draw a picture to solve the problem.

There are seven bears. Each bear wears a hat. How many hats are there?

_____

There are _____ hats.

Problem Solving

Directions: Read the problem. Solve the problem. Circle your answer.

Problem: There are nine flowers. Each flower has one leaf. How many leaves are there?

What Do You Know?

Circle the number of flowers.

1   2   3   4   5

6   7   8   9   10

What Is Your Plan?

Draw leaves on the flowers.

Circle the number of leaves.

1   2   3   4   5   6   7   8   9   10

51619—Conquering the Grades

Directions: Find out about your family. Draw pictures of your family members below.

My Family

Directions: Follow the steps in this experiment to discover how the weather changes.

What You Need

an outdoor thermometer

What to Do

1. Look out the window in the morning.

2. Draw the weather you see. Use the chart below.

3. Put the thermometer outside. Write the temperature in the chart.

4. Repeat in the afternoon.

Morning Weather	Morning Temperature	Afternoon Weather	Afternoon Temperature

5. How did the weather change between the morning and the afternoon?

_____

_____

Directions: Read the clues. Write the name of each person.

Clues

- The youngest daughter is Mary.
- The mother is Madison.
- The oldest daughter is Morgan.
- The grandmother is May.

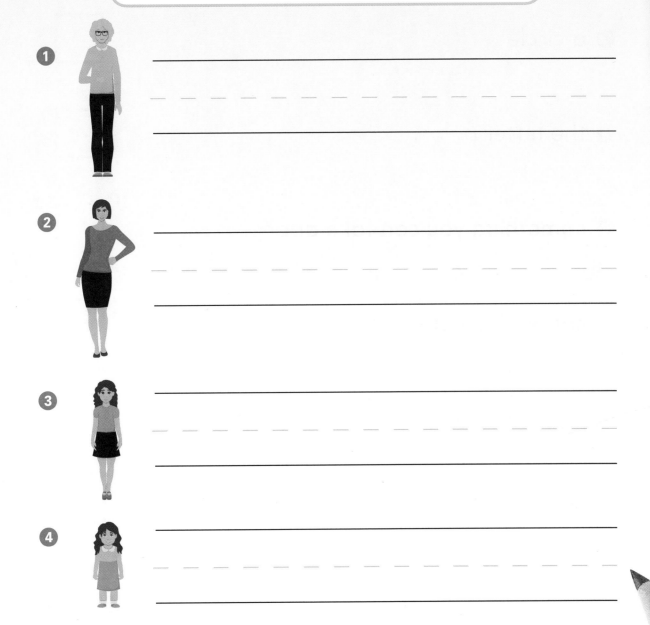

1 _____

2 _____

3 _____

4 _____

Game

Directions: Go on a scavenger hunt at home. Find the things on the list. Mark an *X* in the box when you find **each** thing. If you can, take a picture of it.

❶ the number 6

❷ something that starts with *t*

❸ a circle

❹ the letter *b*

❺ something you can take apart

❻ something cold

❼ the word *and*

❽ four of the same item

Directions: Choose the word with a capital letter. Write it on the line.

1   _____

_____ dog is fast.

(**The** or **the**)

2   _____

_____ pan is hot.

(**A** or **a**)

3   _____

_____ go to bed.

(**we** or **We**)

4   _____

_____ you go?

(**can** or **Can**)

5   _____

_____ have a dog.

(**I** or **i**)

Directions: Trace the words that are about police officers.

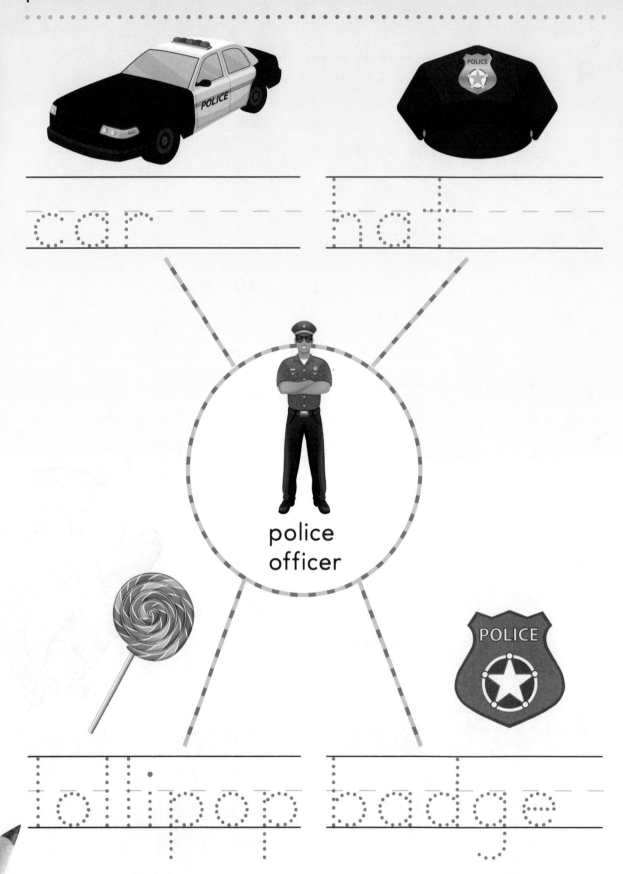

car   hat

police
officer

lollipop badge

Directions: Write about police officers. Fill in the checklist.

Topic

_____

Police officers _____ .

(**save** or **help**)

Detail

_____

They _____

_____

_____ .

Closing

_____

Police officers are _____ .

(**kind** or **brave**)

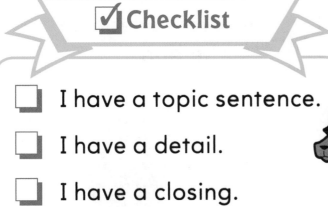 ✓ **Checklist**

☐ I have a topic sentence.

☐ I have a detail.

☐ I have a closing.

Directions: Solve each problem.

1 Draw 1 string on the kite.

4 Color 4 apples.

2 Draw 2 legs on the person.

5 Draw more circles to make a set of 5.

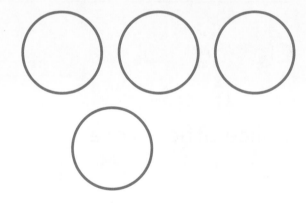

3 Color 3 blocks.

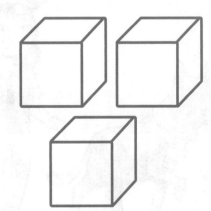

6 Draw 6 legs on the bug.

Directions: Solve each problem.

1 Circle the name of the shapes.

rectangles   pentagons   circles

2 Circle the name of the shapes.

squares   rectangles   hexagons

3 Circle the name of the shapes.

triangles   circles   squares

4 Circle the name of the shapes.

squares   triangles   pentagons

5 Draw an oval. Then, draw a rectangle to the right of the oval.

Directions: Look at the example. Draw lines to solve the problem. Circle your answer.

Example: Which group has more?

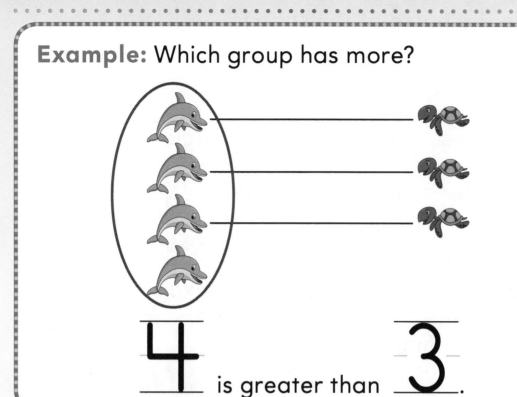

___4___ is greater than ___3___.

Which group has more?

_____ _____

_____ is greater than _____.

Directions: Draw a picture to show the problem. Write your answer.

Ken has 2 apples. Rick has 4 apples. Who has more apples?

Ken

apples

Rick

apples

_____

_____ has more apples.

Directions: Draw lines to match the workers with the goods or services they provide.

Directions: Follow the steps in this experiment to see how you push, pull, and twist.

What You Need

plastic screw-top containers

What to Do

1 Stand facing a partner, toe to toe. Gently push each other on the shoulder. What happens?

_____

- - - - - - - - - - - - - - - - - -

_____

2 What happens when you gently pull each other?

_____

- - - - - - - - - - - - - - - - - -

_____

3 Twist the screw-top container. What happens?

_____

- - - - - - - - - - - - - - - - - -

_____

4 Try pushing, pulling, and twisting some things around the room. Draw what happens on a sheet of paper.

Directions: Put an X on the shape that does not belong in each set. Tell a partner what is the same about the rest of the set.

1

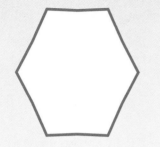  

2

  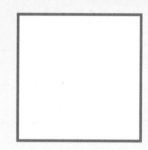

3

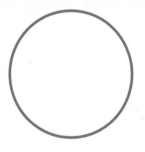  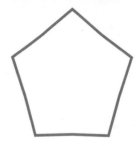

4

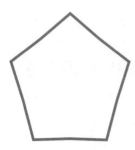  

51619—*Conquering the Grades*

© *Shell Education*

Directions: Play with a partner. Follow the steps.

1 Draw these shapes each on a slip of paper: circle, triangle, square, rectangle, oval, diamond, pentagon, and hexagon.

2 Put the slips into a jar.

3 Sit back to back. Choose a slip of paper without looking.

4 Tell your partner how to draw the shape without saying its name. For example, *This shape has 4 sides. The sides are all equal.*

5 Your partner should draw what he or she hears.

6 Switch roles. Now, your partner should choose a shape, and you should draw. Play until all shapes have been drawn.

Extension Activities

High-Frequency Words Activity

Fill a zip-top bag with a few tablespoons of colored hair gel or paint. Squeeze out all the air, and lay the bag flat on a table. Have your child practice writing the high-frequency words from page 24 on the bag.

Writing Activity

Have your child review his or her writing from page 27. Have him or her circle the first letter of each sentence to make sure it begins with a capital letter.

Mathematics Activity

Help your child make a list of shapes. Include pictures and the names of the shapes. Then, have your child go on a shape hunt around your house. Have him or her put a tally mark next to the picture of the shape each time a shape is found.

Social Studies Activity

Help your child talk to a community worker. Have your child ask the worker about his or her job.

Science Activity

Talk about the experiment from page 33 with your child. Ask him or her which things were hard to push, pull, and twist. Ask your child how these things are similar to and different from each other.

Listening-and-Speaking Activity

Ask your child whether he or she would like to be a police officer. Ask him or her to explain why or why not.

Directions: Match each words to the pictures.

mug   hut   tug

1 hut

2 mug

3 tug

Directions: Circle the word for the picture. Write the word.

4

cup   nut

_____ _____ _____

_ _

_____ _____ _____

UNIT 3

Reading

Directions: Match the words to the pictures.

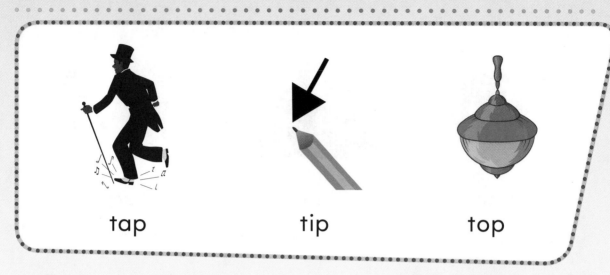

tap   tip   top

1 top

2 tap

3 tip

Directions: Circle the word for the picture. Write the word.

4

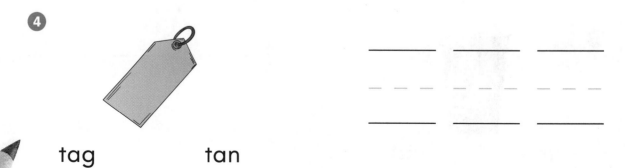

tag   tan

___ ___ ___

51619—Conquering the Grades

Directions: Circle the correct spelling of the word. Trace over the word with a crayon.

1 this

this   thes   tis

2 he

he   hi   hee

3 was

wuz   waz   was

4 for

fore   for   fur

5 on

on   un   onn

Directions: Draw one more picture in each category.

Fruit

Animals

Clothes

Sports

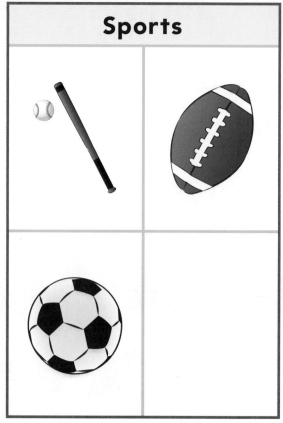

51619—Conquering the Grades

Directions: Circle the picture you like best. Write your opinion. Write a reason.

summer

winter

Opinion

_____

- - - - - - - - - - - - - - - - - - - -

I like _____ .

Reason

_____

- - - - - - - - - - - - - - - - - - - -

I like it because _____

_____

- - - - - - - - - - - - - - - - - - - -

_____

_____

_____ .

Directions: Write about summer or winter. Fill in the checklist.

Opinion

_____

_____ is the best season.

(**Summer** or **Winter**)

Reason

_____

I like it because _____

_____

_____ .

Closing

_____

I love _____ !

(**summer** or **winter**)

☑ **Checklist**

☐ I state my opinion.

☐ I have a reason.

☐ I have a closing.

Directions: Draw a picture to solve the problem.

Kenny picks 7 flowers. He picks 1 more. How many flowers does he have now?

_____

Kenny has _____ flowers now.

Directions: Read the problem. Solve the problem. Circle your answer.

Problem: Tom has 4 blocks. Sue gives him 1 more. How many blocks does Tom have now?

What Do You Know?

Draw a picture to show the problem.

What Is Your Plan?

Count the blocks.

Circle the number of blocks.

1   2   3   4   5   6   7   8   9   10

Directions: Draw a picture to show what each person has the authority to do.

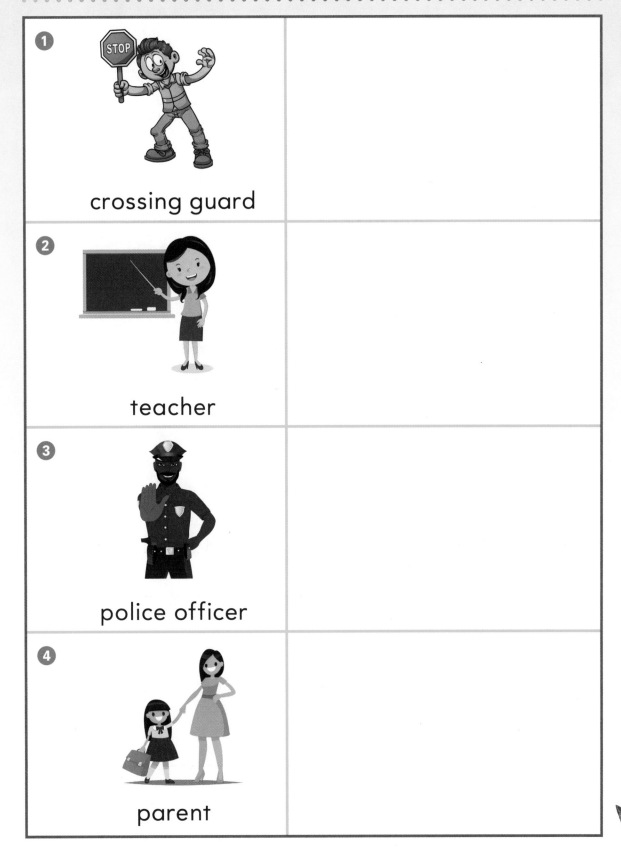

1 crossing guard	
2 teacher	
3 police officer	
4 parent	

Directions: Follow the steps in this experiment to discover how seeds are different.

What You Need

- lots of different seeds
- jar with lid

What to Do

1 Put all the seeds in a jar.

2 Choose a seed. Take it out, and look at it carefully.

3 Draw a picture of your seed below.

4 Put the seed back into the jar. Shake the seeds.

5 Try to find your seed again. How do you know it's the same seed?

_____

- -

_____

_____

_____

Directions: Draw a picture of a food that begins with each letter listed.

1 B

2 N

3 S

4 P

5 G

6 L

7 C

8 D

Directions: Play with a partner. Place a paper clip over the X. Place a pencil in the middle of the paper clip to make a spinner. Take turns flicking the spinner. Count out the number of beans or other counters that matches your spin. Keep playing until someone has at least 20 counters.

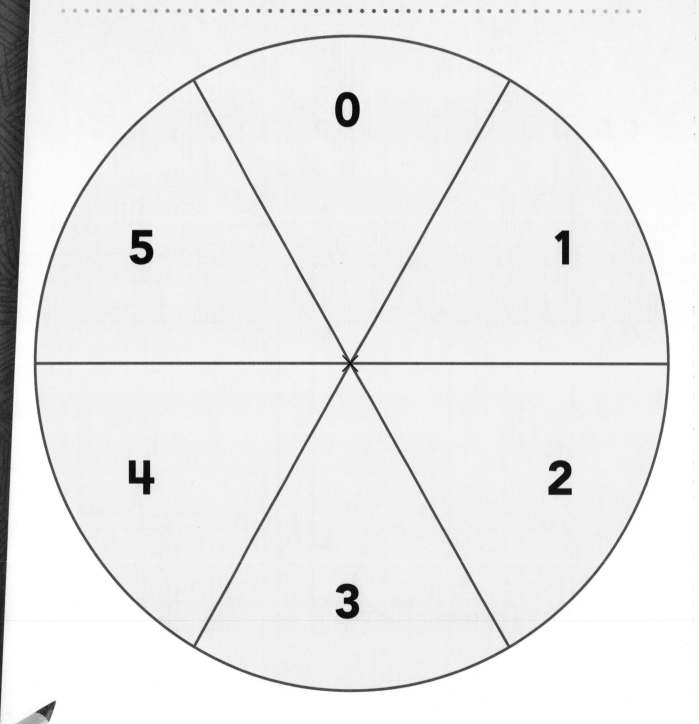

High-Frequency Words Activity

Review the high-frequency words on page 39 with your child. Cut out the letters for the words from advertisements, catalogs, or packages. Have your child glue the letters on a sheet of paper to spell each word.

Writing Activity

Ask your child to think of one more reason he or she likes summer or winter. Have your child write his or her reason on a sheet of paper. Or write your child's reason in large printing, and have him or her trace over your letters.

Mathematics Activity

Practice counting objects with your child while you are driving. Decide on an object, such as stop signs. Work together to count the number of objects you see while driving around town.

Social Studies Activity

Have your child draw a picture of another person who has authority in the community.

Critical-Thinking Activity

Ask your child to name foods that begin with other letters of the alphabet. Or, select a different category, such as clothing or games.

Listening-and-Speaking Activity

Ask your child to name the authority figures in his or her life. Ask your child to explain why those people are important.

Directions: Match the words to the pictures.

bat   bit   bet

① bat

② bet

③ bit

Directions: Circle the word for the picture. Write the word.

④

Ben   bug

_____ _____ _____

- - - - - - - - - - - -

_____ _____ _____

Directions: Match the words to the pictures.

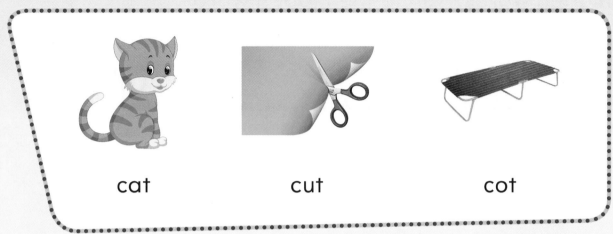

cat   cut   cot

1 cot

2 cut

3 cat

Directions: Circle the word for the picture. Write the word.

4

can   cap

_____ _____ _____

_____ _____ _____

_____ _____ _____

APC

High-Frequency Words

Directions: Read the words in the box. Find the hidden words. Circle the hidden words.

| are | have | with | his | they |

1. l r a t i a r e m e s a

2. h w i t h w t s k l m t

3. y e c s l h y a t h e y

4. p m r s i h a v e n p a

5. r s a h v h i s h s e s

Directions: Write the opposite of each word. Use the words in the box to help you.

go　　big　　top　　hot　　up

1  ↓

down _____

2  cold _____

3  little _____

4  stop _____

5  bottom _____

Writing

Directions: Think about a time you did something with your friends. Draw notes about the day.

Who?

Where?

When?

Event 1

Event 2

Directions: Write about a day with your friends. Fill in the checklist.

Introduction

_____

I spent a day with _____ .

Events

_____

First, _____ .
_____

Then, _____ .

Closing Sentence

_____

_____

_____ ,

and I had a great day!

☑ Checklist

- ☐ I have an introduction.
- ☐ I have events.
- ☐ I have a closing.

Directions: Solve each problem.

① Circle the group that has more fish.

③ Put an X on the group that has more.

② Circle the box with fewer flowers.

④ Circle the bowl that has more fish.

Directions: Solve each problem.

1 How many pumpkins are there?

9   10   11

2 Circle the machine with 11 pieces of gum.

3 How many ants are there?

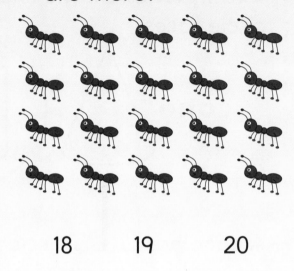

18   19   20

4 Circle 16 fish.

Mathematics

51619—Conquering the Grades

Directions: Look at the example. Solve the problem.

Example: Circle the shape that has more circle faces.

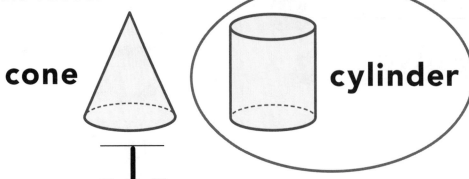

cone

cylinder

A cone has __1__ circle face.

A cylinder has __2__ circle faces.

Circle the shape that has more faces.

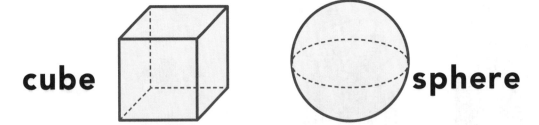

cube

sphere

a cube has _____ faces

a sphere has _____ faces

Directions: Trace the pictures to solve each problem.

How many corners do these shapes have? Circle the corners

1

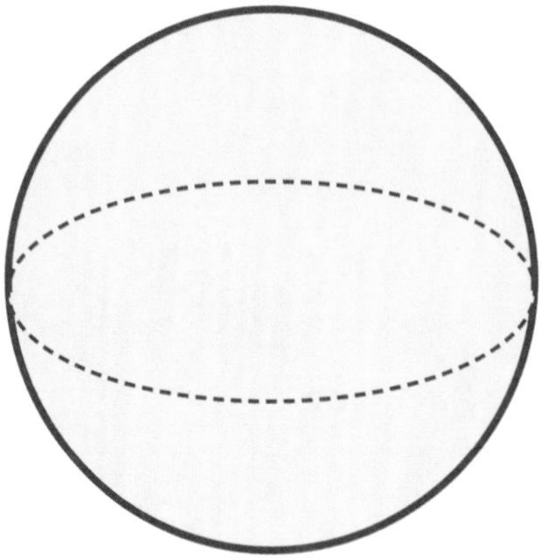

_____ corners

2

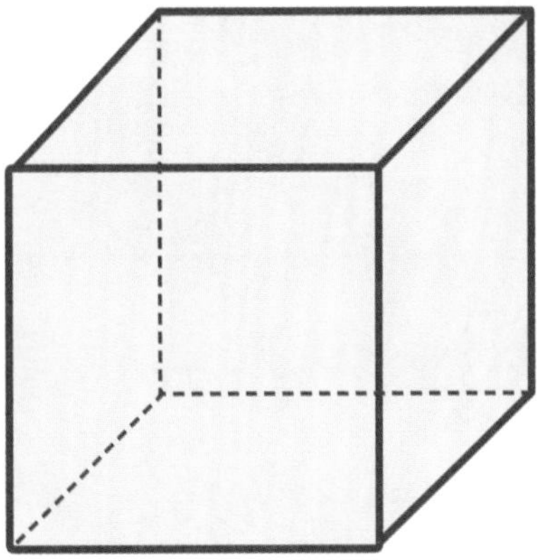

_____ corners

3

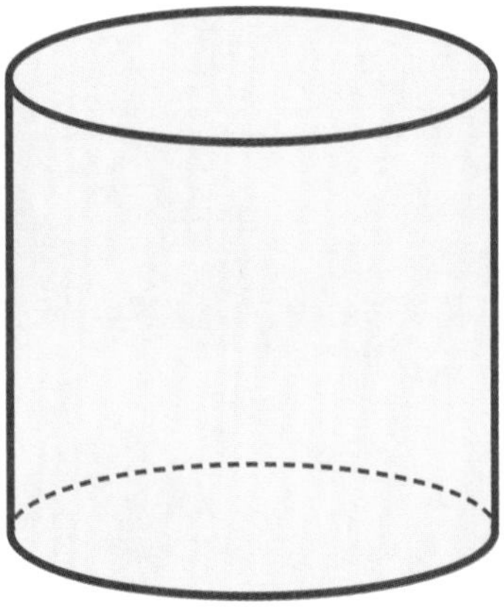

_____ corners

Directions: Make a time line of your day. Draw what you do during each part of the day.

My Day

Morning
Noon
Evening
Night

Directions: Follow the steps in this experiment to discover how balls move.

What You Need

balls of different sizes

What to Do

1. Choose one ball. Think about the different ways you make balls move in the games you play.

2. See what happens when you:
   - flick it with a finger
   - roll it
   - throw it underarm
   - bounce it
   - pat it

3. Pick another ball. Move this ball in the same ways. Think about how this ball moves.

Directions: Find objects that look like the ones shown. Answer *yes* or *no* for each question.

Shape	Will it stack?	Will it slide?	Will it roll?

Directions: Place a paper clip over the X. Place a pencil through the paper clip to make a spinner. Play with a partner. Each player rolls a ball. Spin the spinner. If your ball matches your spin, you get a point. Reroll the balls, but let the second player spin this time. Tally your points in the chart. The first person to get 10 points wins.

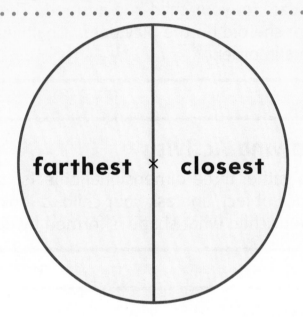

farthest ✗ closest

Player 1: _____

Player 2: _____

Extension Activities

High-Frequency Words Activity

Have your child form letters with modeling clay to spell the high-frequency words on page 54.

Writing Activity

Arrange a play date for your child and a friend. Then, ask your child what he or she did on the play date. Challenge your child to list the events in order.

Problem-Solving Activity

Help your child gather three-dimensional objects. Shine a flashlight on each object, and ask your child to look at its shadow. Ask your child what shape is formed by each shadow.

Science Activity

Talk to your child about the experiment on page 63. Ask your child to compare how the two different balls moved. What was the same? What was different?

Critical-Thinking Activity

Show your child a cone-shaped object. Ask him or her whether it will stack, slide, or roll.

Listening-and-Speaking Activity

Ask your child how a time line for his or her day would be different during the week and during the weekend.

Directions: Match the words to the pictures.

fist   sing   crib

1 crib

2 fist

3 sing

Directions: Circle the word for the picture. Write the word.

4

_____ _____ _____ _____

_____ _____ _____ _____

mist   lift

Directions: Match the words to the pictures.

stop   chop   lock

1 stop

2 lock

3 chop

Directions: Circle the word for the picture. Write the word.

4

dock   crop

_____ _____ _____ _____

- - - - - - - - - - - - - -

_____ _____ _____

Directions: Trace each word. Then, write each word twice.

1

2

3

4

5

Directions: Write each lowercase letter.

1 B _____

5 I _____

2 E _____

6 R _____

3 G _____

7 T _____

4 H _____

8 Y _____

Directions: Trace the words about features of Earth.

mountain

lake

Earth

hill

glacier

Directions: Write about Earth. Fill in the checklist.

Topic

_____

Earth has _____ features.

(a lot of or **many)**

Detail

_____

Earth has _____

_____

_____.

Closing

_____

Earth is _____.

 ✓ **Checklist**

☐ I have a topic sentence.

☐ I have a detail.

☐ I have a closing.

Directions: Solve each problem.

1 Circle the number that is one more than 4.

3   4   5

2 Circle the number that comes after 6.

3   5   7

3 I am the number that comes after 8. What number am I?

_____

_____

4 I am the number that comes after 5. What number am I?

_____

_____

5 John finds 4 seashells. Then, he finds one more. How many seashells does he have now?

_____

_____

_____

6 Sandy started counting like this:

1   2   3   4   5

How is Sandy counting? Circle the answer.

forward   backward

Mathematics

Directions: Solve each problem.

1 Circle the container that holds the most.

2 Circle the container that holds the most.

3 Circle the object that weighs the least.

4 Circle the shortest animal

5 Draw or write something that weighs less than a boy.

6 Draw a container that holds more than a bucket.

Directions: Look at the example. Solve the problem. Circle your answer.

Example: Count the berries. Start at 5. How many berries are there in all?

1   2   3   4   5   6   7   ⑧   9   10

Count the crayons. Start at 3. How many crayons are there in all?

1   2   3   4   5   6   7   8   9   10

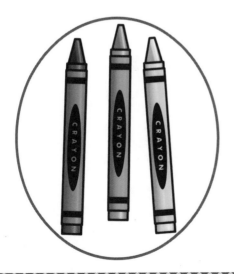 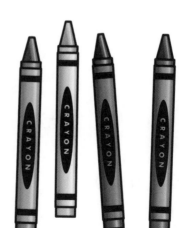

Directions: Draw a picture to show the problem. Circle your answer.

Draw 2 more bugs. Count the bugs. Start at 3. How many bugs are there in all?

3

Circle the answer.

1   2   3   4   5   6   7   8   9   10

Directions: Draw each natural feature.

river	mountain
hill	**lake**

Directions: Follow the steps in this experiment to discover how animals live.

What You Need

an animal to observe
(such as a bird, an ant, or a lizard)

What to Do

1 Find an animal to observe. Observe it for a few minutes.

2 Draw a picture of where the animal lives.

3 Tell about what the animal is doing.

_____

_____

_____

_____

Directions: Sort the letters. Put some in the first box. Put some in the second box. Tell a partner how you sorted the letters.

| a | c | e | h | k | m | p | s | v | z |

| | |
| | |

51619—Conquering the Grades

Directions: Play with a partner. Do a scavenger hunt around the house. Look for the letters in the charts below. Each player should tally the letters he or she finds. The person with the most tallies at the end of five minutes wins.

Player 1		Player 2	
B		B	
E		E	
G		G	
H		H	
M		M	
R		R	
T		T	
Y		Y	

51619—*Conquering the Grades*   © *Shell Education*

High-Frequency Words Activity

Have your child practice spelling the high-frequency words from page 69 in different silly voices.

Writing Activity

Have your child review his or her writing from page 72. Have him or her circle the first letter of each sentence to make sure it begins with a capital letter.

Mathematics Activity

Help your child gather two containers of different sizes. Help him or her find a way to prove that one container holds more than the other container.

Problem-Solving Activity

Put some counters, such as buttons, beans, or O-shaped cereal into a container. Have your child grab a small handful and count the objects. Then, have him or her grab another handful and count on.

Science Activity

Have your child observe a different animal. Ask your child to compare this animal to the one he or she observed in the experiment on page 78.

Listening-and-Speaking Activity

Ask your child to name the natural features that you have in your local area or that you have visited. Ask your child how these features are different.

Directions: Read the text. Answer the questions on the next page.

Gus and His Pets

Gus has two pets.

Gus can run and jump with one pet.

Ruff! Ruff!

One pet does not run or jump.

Quack! Quack!

51619—Conquering the Grades   © *Shell Education*

Directions: Listen to and read "Gus and His Pets." Answer the questions.

1 Who has pets?

Ⓐ a pup

Ⓑ a duck

Ⓒ Gus

2 What kinds of pets does Gus have?

Ⓐ a pup and a duck

Ⓑ a bug and a pup

Ⓒ a duck and a cat

3 Which pet runs?

Ⓐ a pup

Ⓑ a duck

Ⓒ a bug

4 Which is another good title?

Ⓐ "Duck in the Pond"

Ⓑ "Two Pets"

Ⓒ "Gus Runs"

Directions: Trace each word. Read each sentence. Circle the word in each sentence.

1 from

It is from mom.

2 or

Do you like blue or red?

3 one

He has one truck.

4 had

I had a good day.

5 by

Sit by me.

Directions: Circle the noun in each sentence.

1 A boy digs.

2 The lamp is red.

3 A dog runs fast.

4 The girl plays with a toy.

5 The cat is slow.

6 The desk is full.

Directions: Circle the picture you like best. Write your opinion. Write a reason.

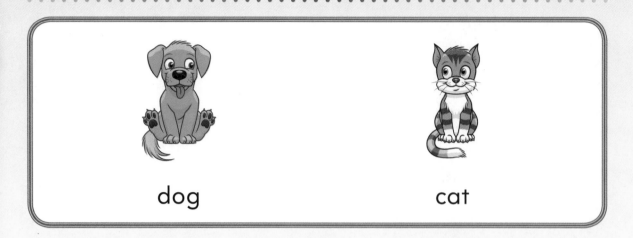

dog

cat

Opinion

_____

I like _____ .

Reason

_____

I like it because _____

_____

_____ .

Directions: Write about a dog or a cat. Fill in the checklist.

Opinion

_____

- -

_____ is the best pet.

(**A dog** or **A cat**)

Reason

_____

- -

I like it because _____

_____

- -

_____ .

Closing

_____

- -

I love _____ .

(**dogs** or **cats**)

☑ Checklist

- ☐ I state my opinion.
- ☐ I have a reason.
- ☐ I have a closing.

Directions: Solve each problem by adding.

1

_____

3 + 2 = _____

4

_____

2 + 2 = _____

2

_____

1 + 3 = _____

5

_____

2 + 3 = _____

3

_____

4 + 1 = _____

6

_____

1 + 3 = _____

Directions: Solve each problem.

① Does the solid have any flat surfaces? Circle the answer.

yes   no

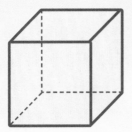

④ Does the solid have any curved surfaces? Circle the answer.

yes   no

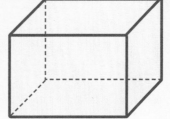

② How many corners does a hexagon have?

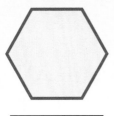

_____

_____

⑤ How many corners does a circle have?

_____

_____

③ Circle the shape with 3 sides.

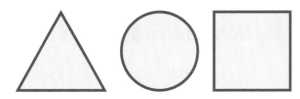

⑥ Color the shapes with 4 sides.

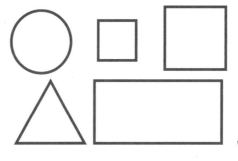

Directions: Read the problem. Solve the problem.

Jess has 3 cats. Bob has 1 cat. Leo has 4 cats. Who has the most cats? Who has the fewest cats?

Draw a picture to show the problem.

_____

_____ has the most cats.

_____

_____ has the fewest cats.

Directions: Read the problem. Solve the problem.

There are 4 slices of pizza in a box. Tom eats 2 slices. Maria eats 1 slice. How many slices of pizza are in the box now?

Draw a picture to show the problem.

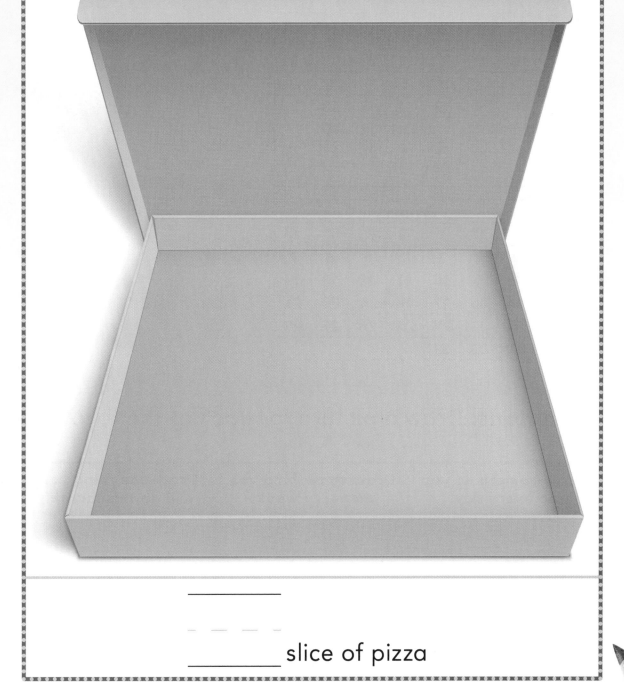

_____

_____ slice of pizza

Directions: Draw lines to match the calendars to the correct words.

1

January						
S	M	T	W	Th	F	S
1	2	3	4	5	6	7
8	9	10	11	12	**13**	14
15	16	17	18	19	20	21
22	23	24	25	26	27	28
29	30	31				

month

2

January						
S	M	T	W	Th	F	S
1	2	3	4	5	6	7
8	**9**	**10**	**11**	**12**	**13**	**14**
15	16	17	18	19	20	21
22	23	24	25	26	27	28
29	30	31				

day

3

January						
S	M	T	W	Th	F	S
1	**2**	**3**	**4**	**5**	**6**	**7**
8	**9**	**10**	**11**	**12**	**13**	**14**
15	**16**	**17**	**18**	**19**	**20**	**21**
22	**23**	**24**	**25**	**26**	**27**	**28**
29	**30**	**31**				

week

Directions: Draw a picture for each of the following.

Draw something you do every day.	Draw something you do every week.	Draw one thing you will do this month.

Directions: Follow the steps in this experiment to discover how the weather changes.

What to Do

1 Look outside each day.

2 Choose a symbol for each kind of weather. Use your symbols to draw the weather in the chart each day.

Monday	Tuesday	Wednesday	Thursday	Friday

3 How did the weather change this week?

_____

- -

_____

_____

- -

_____

Directions: Each row must have each shape ♡ ☺.
Each column much have each shape ♡ ☺.

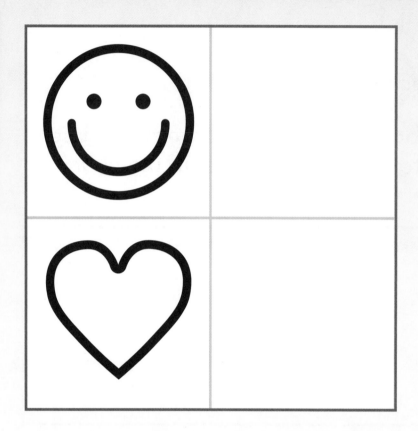

51619—Conquering the Grades

Directions: Play with a partner. Put a paper clip on the X. Put a pencil through the paper clip to make a spinner. Put 20 small objects into a bag. Each player reaches into the bag and pulls out some objects. Then, spin the spinner. If your objects match the spin, you get a point. Put the objects back, and start again. Take turns until someone gets 10 points.

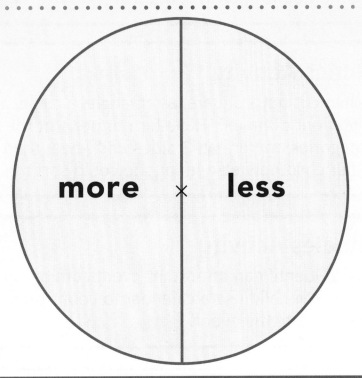

Points	
Player 1:	**Player 2:**

High-Frequency Words Activity

Review the high-frequency words on page 84 with your child. Have him or her write the words with sidewalk chalk on the sidewalk or driveway.

Writing Activity

Help your child review his or her writing from page 87. Have him or her circle the nouns in each sentence.

Mathematics Activity

Help your child cut out a square, a rectangle, a circle, a triangle, and a hexagon out of paper. Have him or her sort the shapes into two categories: more than 3 sides and fewer than 3 sides. Then, ask your child how else he or she could sort the shapes.

Social Studies Activity

Help your child identify an important event coming up, such as a holiday. Have your child use a calendar to count the number of days and weeks until the event.

Science Activity

Have your child track the weather during a different week. If possible, choose a week with much different weather. Ask your child how the weather is different from the first week he or she observed.

Listening-and-Speaking Activity

Ask your child why he or she prefers dogs or cats. Ask your child what he or she would say to convince a person who disagreed with his or her opinion.

Directions: Read the text. Answer the questions on the next page.

A Hen

This is a hen.

The baby is a chick.

They live in a pen.

They peck for seeds and corn.

Directions: Listen to and read "A Hen." Answer the questions.

1 What is the baby called?
- Ⓐ a hen
- Ⓑ a kid
- Ⓒ a chick

2 Where do the hens live?
- Ⓐ in a box
- Ⓑ in the dirt
- Ⓒ in a pen

3 How do hens get seeds and corn?
- Ⓐ They dig.
- Ⓑ They peck.
- Ⓒ They hunt.

4 What is this text about?
- Ⓐ pens
- Ⓑ hens
- Ⓒ seeds and corn

51619—Conquering the Grades   *© Shell Education*

Directions: Look at the shape of the word. Find the box with that shape. Write each letter in a box.

not	but	what	we

Example:

①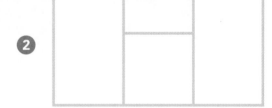

②

③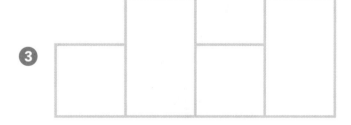

④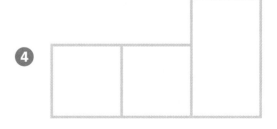

51619—Conquering the Grades

Language

Directions: Add punctuation.

1 I like the pink cap

6 Why did you go

2 Who will win

7 I love to read

3 The tent is wet

8 The pen is blue

4 Do not yell

5 Who can mop

Directions: Think about a time you went to a birthday party. Draw notes about the day.

Writing

Who?	Where?

When?	Event 1

Event 2

Directions: Write about a birthday party. Fill in the checklist.

Introduction

I went to a birthday party for

_____

- -

_____ .

Events

_____

- -

First, _____ .

- -

Then, _____ .

Closing Sentence

_____

- -

_____

had a great birthday!

☑ **Checklist**

- ☐ I have an introduction.
- ☐ I have events.
- ☐ I have a closing.

Directions: Solve each problem.

1 How many rings are there?

14   15   16

2 How many snails are there?

17   18   19

3 How many bugs are there?

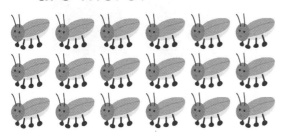

18   19   20

4 Color 10 balls.

5 Circle 14 bees.

6 Circle 13 sea stars.

Mathematics

Directions: Solve each problem by subtracting.

1

_____

3 – 2 = _____

4

_____

3 – 0 = _____

2

_____

5 – 3 = _____

5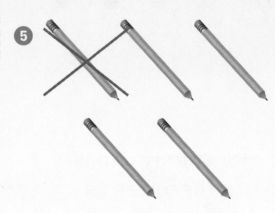

_____

5 – 1 = _____

3

_____

6 – 5 = _____

6

_____

5 – 5 = _____

Directions: Read the problem. Solve the problem.

There are 8 frogs on a log. Two frogs are green. One frog is orange. The rest of the frogs are red. How many frogs are red?

Draw a picture to show the problem.

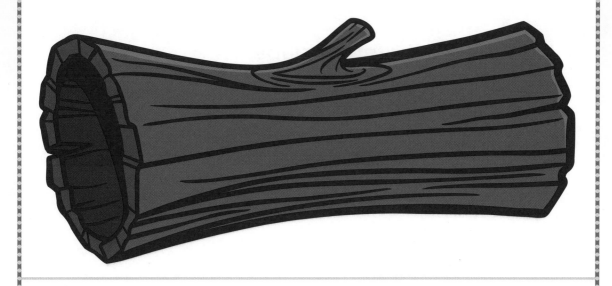

_____

2 + 1 + _____ = 8

_____

There are _____ red frogs.

Directions: Read the problem. Solve the problem.

Kai wants to sort leaves by size.

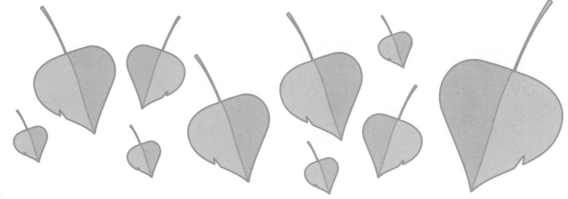

❶ How many groups should Kai make?

_____

_____

_____

❷ Sort the leaves into groups.

❸ Which group has the fewest leaves? Circle the group.

❹ Which group has the most leaves? Write an X on the group.

Directions: Write the names of the American symbols. Color the symbols.

American Symbols

- bald eagle
- American flag
- Statue of Liberty
- Liberty Bell

1 _____

2 _____

3 _____

4 _____

Directions: Follow the steps in this experiment to see how objects roll.

What You Need

- objects
- board
- newspaper
- paint

What to Do

1. Angle the board with some books or a rock. You have made a ramp.

2. Cover the ramp with newspaper. Place newspaper around the ramp, especially at the bottom.

3. Paint one side of an object. Let it go down the ramp.

4. Repeat step #3 with two more objects. Use different colors of paint on each one. Watch them go down the ramp.

5. Draw how they went down the ramp.

Directions: Write the name of each baby animal. Use word clues to help you.

Baby Animals

- piglet
- owlet
- chick
- spiderling
- joey
- pup

①

_____

④

_____

②

_____

⑤

_____

③

_____

⑥

_____

Directions: Play with a partner. Place a paper clip on the X. Place a pencil through the paper clip to make a spinner. Take turns spinning the spinner. Read the word it lands on. Place a check mark next to the word in your chart. The first player to get two check marks next to each word wins.

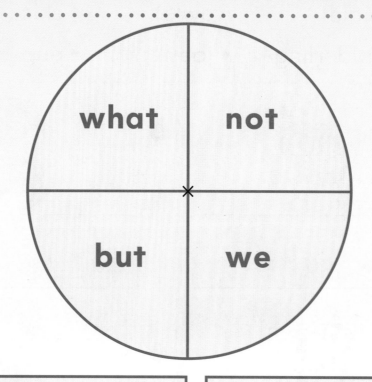

Player 1	
what	
not	
but	
we	

Player 1	
what	
not	
but	
we	

Directions: Write the verb.

_____

1 The bug _____ .

(**rug** or **ran**)

_____

2 The baby _____ .

(**dad** or **naps**)

_____

3 Mom will _____ it.

(**cat** or **fix**)

_____

4 The man _____ me.

(**helps** or **hand**)

_____

5 Tim _____ the pen.

(**gum** or **grabs**)

Directions: Trace the words about ducks.

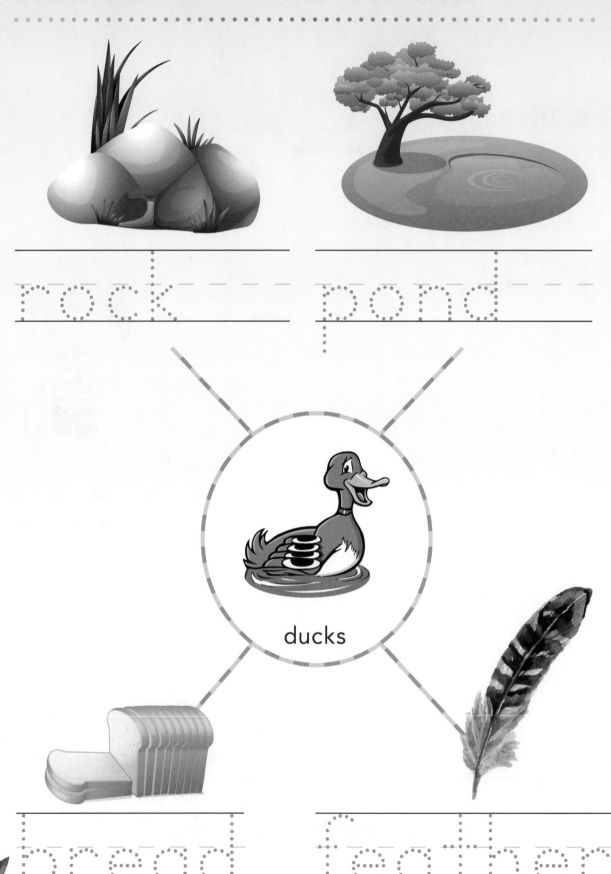

rock   pond

ducks

bread   feather

Directions: Write about ducks. Fill in the checklist.

Topic

_____

Ducks are _____ .

Detail

_____

They _____

_____

_____ .

Closing

_____

I love _____ .

 **Checklist**

☐ I have a topic sentence.

☐ I have a detail.

☐ I have a closing.

Directions: Solve each problem.

1 Count the donuts. Draw an equal set of circles.

2 Draw a set of 2 triangles. Draw a set of more than 2 circles.

2
More than 2

3 Count the balloons. Draw a set of circles that is more than the balloons.

4 Color an equal number of circles.

Directions: Solve each problem.

1

_____ _____ _____

\- - - + - - - = - - -

_____ _____ _____

3 Circle the number sentence that matches the picture.

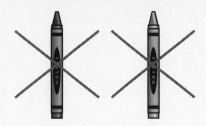

2 + 2 = 4

2 – 0 = 2

2 – 2 = 0

2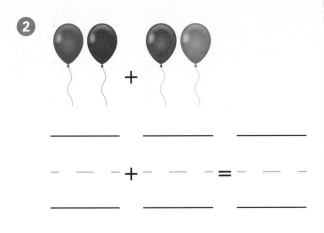

_____ _____ _____

\- - - + - - - = - - -

_____ _____ _____

4 Draw a picture to show 1 + 1 = 2

Directions: Read the problem. Solve the problem.

There are 10 beads in a bag. Deanne has 90 beads in all. How many bags does she have?

Draw a picture to show the problem.

_____

_ _ _ _ _

_____ bags

51619—Conquering the Grades   © *Shell Education*

Directions: Read the problem. Solve the problem.

❶ Draw an object that is long and light.

❷ Draw an object that is short and heavy.

❸ Draw an object that is long and heavy.

❹ Draw an object that is short and light.

Directions: Color the things that are *needs*. Circle the things that are *wants*.

51619—Conquering the Grades © *Shell Education*

Directions: Follow the steps in this experiment to discover how you can group rocks.

What You Need

- lots of rocks
- magnifying glass
- water
- shallow bowl

What to Do

1. Look at the rocks. Use a magnifying glass to look closely.

2. Put the rocks into three groups: small, bigger, and biggest. Draw them in the boxes.

Small Rocks	Bigger Rocks	Biggest Rocks

3. Put the rocks into a bowl. Pour some water on them.

4. Put the wet rocks into groups of different colors. Tell a family member about the groups you made.

Directions: Think about each object in the box. Write the objects in the orders listed.

| ruler | ant | door | mug |

1 Shortest to Tallest

_____   _____

_____   _____

_____   _____

2 Lightest to Heaviest

_____   _____

_____   _____

_____   _____

Directions: Play with a partner. Take turns rolling two number cubes. Add the dots on both cubes. Cross off the sum in your box. The first player to cross off all the numbers wins. Play two times.

Player 1: _____

| 7 | 8 | 9 | 10 | 11 | 12 |

Player 2: _____

| 7 | 8 | 9 | 10 | 11 | 12 |

Player 1: _____

| 7 | 8 | 9 | 10 | 11 | 12 |

Player 2: _____

| 7 | 8 | 9 | 10 | 11 | 12 |

High-Frequency Words Activity

Have your child use cereal pieces to form the letters of each high-frequency word from page 114. Have him or her practice reading the words. Then, he or she can eat the words!

Writing Activity

Help your child review his or her writing from page 117. Ask your child to identify the verbs he or she wrote. Have your child act out each verb.

Problem-Solving Activity

Talk to your child about comparisons. Have your child name objects that are taller, shorter, lighter, and heavier than himself or herself.

Social Studies Activity

Ask your child to think about the things he or she uses every day. Ask your child which are needs and which are wants.

Critical-Thinking Activity

Review the activity on page 124 with your child. Choose three new objects, and have your child repeat the activity. Discuss why the lists for tallest and heaviest may differ.

Listening-and-Speaking Activity

Ask your child to explain how he or she sorted the rocks in the science experiment on page 123.

Directions: Read the text. Answer the questions on the next page.

The Ox

An ox can pull a rock.

It can pull a log.

It can help with a crop.

An ox is strong!

Directions: Listen to and read "The Ox." Answer the questions.

1 What animal is this story about?

(A) an ox

(B) a log

(C) a cat

2 What can an ox pull?

(A) a crop

(B) a rock

(C) a baby

3 Who does the ox help?

(A) the rock

(B) a farmer

(C) another ox

4 Which is another good title?

(A) "Strong Ox"

(B) "Move Rocks"

(C) "Animals"

Directions: Read the words in the box. Find the hidden words. Circle the hidden words.

| use | said | there | an | each |

1. t u d k e h k a n w t d e t h

2. s r i u s e q u j e z h p e i b

3. w e n b u x v d e a c h i n z

4. a i n b n s a i d k m i p u r w

5. d k i p q u g t h e r e i e o h a

Directions: Circle the words that are spelled correctly.

1. rak
   (rake)

2. (rat)
   ratt

3. tope
   top

4. het
   hit

5. bike
   bice

Directions: Circle the picture you like best. Write your opinion. Write a reason.

ice cream   a cookie

Opinion

_____

I like _____ .

Reason

_____

I like it because _____

_____

_____

_____

_____ .

Directions: Write about ice cream or cookies. Fill in the checklist.

Opinion

_____

_____ is the best.

(**Ice cream** or **A cookie**)

Reason

_____

I like it because _____

_____

_____ .

Closing

_____

I love _____

_____

_____ .

☑ Checklist

☐ I state my opinion.

☐ I have a reason.

☐ I have a closing.

51619–Conquering the Grades   © Shell Education

Directions: Solve each problem.

1 How many sunflowers are there?

_____

2 How many lizards are there?

_____

3 Count how many.

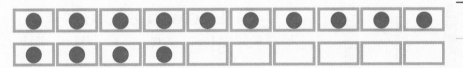

_____

4 How many snails are there?

_____

5 Count how many.

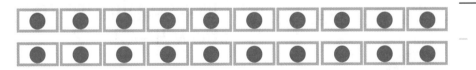

_____

6 Count how many.

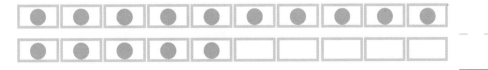

_____

Directions: Solve each problem.

1 How many fish are left?

_____

___ ___ ___

_____

2 How many crayons are left?

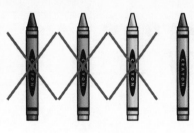

_____

___ ___ ___

_____

3 Circle the number sentence that matches the picture.

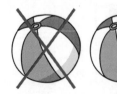

2 – 1 = 1

2 + 1 = 3

3 – 1 = 2

4 Circle the number sentence that matches the picture.

3 + 0 = 3

3 – 3 = 0

3 – 0 = 3

5 Draw a picture to show 5 – 1 = 4.

6 Draw a picture to show 4 – 2 = 2.

Kiki has 4 dresses. Two are green, and the rest are red. How many red dresses does Kiki have?

Draw a picture to show the problem.

Kiki has _____ red dresses.

Directions: Read the problem. Solve the problem.

Mita has 9 balloons. Three are red. Three are yellow. The rest are blue. How many are blue?

Draw a picture to show the problem.

_____

There are _____ blue balloons.

Directions: Draw the job each community helper does.

1 doctor

2 firefighter

3 mail carrier

4 police officer

Directions: Follow this experiment to see what a person needs.

What to Do

1 Observe yourself for a day. Draw pictures of what you need to survive.

air	shelter
food	**water**

2 Could you live without all of the things listed above? Why or why not?

_____

_____

_____

_____

Directions: The same letter is missing in each set of words. Write it on the lines to complete the words.

1
_____

_____at

_____ap

_____amp

2
_____

m _____p

st _____p

n _____d

3
_____

s _____t

b _____t

l _____p

Game

Directions: Play with a partner. Put a paper clip on each X. Put a pencil through each paper clip to make a spinner. Flick each spinner in order. Write the word you spun on a sheet of paper. Take turns making as many words as you can in two minutes. Circle the real words. The person with the most real words wins.

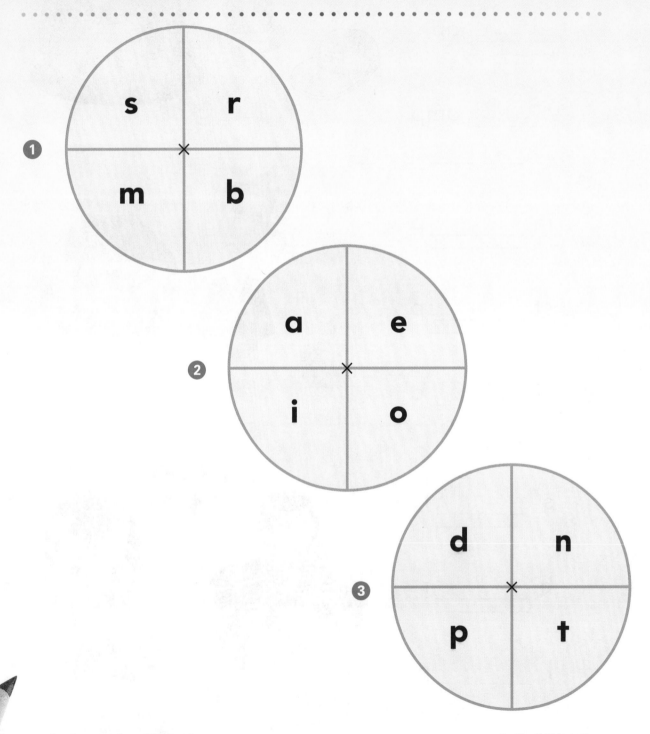

High-Frequency Words Activity

Review the high-frequency words from page 129 with your child. Have him or her write the words using a variety of writing tools, such as a pen, a pencil, paint, a marker, and crayons.

Writing Activity

Revisit page 132. Work with your child to spell as many words as possible correctly. Focus on sight words or spelling rules that your child knows.

Mathematics Activity

Tell your child the ages of three friends or family members. Ask your child whether each age is greater than, less than, or equal to his or her age.

Social Studies Activity

Ask your child to name two other community helpers and discuss the jobs they each do.

Critical-Thinking Activity

Ask your child to brainstorm more words that share one letter. Challenge him or her to think of as many as possible.

Listening-and-Speaking Activity

Ask your child what community helper job he or she would most like to have and why.

Directions: Read the text. Answer the questions on the next page.

Camping

Sam and Pam love to camp at the beach.

They swim.

Dad makes a campfire.

They fix hot dogs.

Yum!

Directions: Listen to and read "Camping." Answer the questions.

1 Who makes the campfire?

   Ⓐ Sam

   Ⓑ Pam

   Ⓒ Dad

2 Where do they camp?

   Ⓐ at the beach

   Ⓑ at the forest

   Ⓒ in the yard

3 How do the hot dogs taste?

   Ⓐ bad

   Ⓑ okay

   Ⓒ very good

4 What is this story about?

   Ⓐ swimming

   Ⓑ camping at the beach

   Ⓒ making hot dogs

Directions: Read the sentences. Circle the high-frequency words in each sentence. Write each word two times.

| which | she | do | how | their |

1 How can we fix this?

_____

- - - - - - - - - - - - - - - - -

_____

2 She is my friend.

_____

- - - - - - - - - - - - - - - - -

_____

3 Their play was good.

_____

- - - - - - - - - - - - - - - - -

_____

4 Which one is bigger?

_____

- - - - - - - - - - - - - - - - -

_____

5 Can you do it?

_____

- - - - - - - - - - - - - - - - -

_____

Directions: Write the plural noun.

1 You have two _____ .

(**dime** or **dimes**)

2 The _____ are red.

(**ant** or **ants**)

3 He has three ice cream _____ .

(**cones** or **cone**)

4 Let's play two _____ .

(**game** or **games**)

5 I see five _____ .

(**lakes** or **lake**)

Directions: Trace the words about washing your hands.

washing your hands

Directions: Write about washing your hands. Fill in the checklist.

Topic

_____

Washing your hands is _____ .

Detail

_____

You must _____

_____

_____ .

Closing

_____

Make sure you _____ .

☑ Checklist

☐ I have a topic sentence.

☐ I have a detail.

☐ I have a closing.

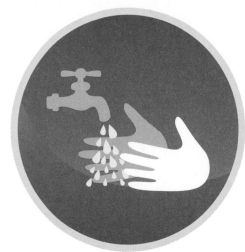

Directions: Solve each problem.

1 Circle the larger number.

5   9

2 Circle the smaller number.

10   8

3 Circle the smaller number.

7   6

4 Circle the larger number.

11   9

5 Circle the smallest number.

5   8   12

6 Circle the largest number.

6   12   16

Directions: Solve each problem.

1 Marcy drinks 3 glasses of water. Later, she drinks 2 more glasses of water. How many glasses of water did Marcy drink?

_____

_____

_____

2 A pizza was cut into 6 pieces. Michelle ate 2 of the pieces. How many pieces are left?

_____

_____

_____

3 Kiko had 3 jackets. She lost one. How many jackets does she still have?

_____

_____

4 Draw a picture to match. There are 3 fish swimming. Then, 2 more fish come.

Directions: Read the problem. Solve the problem. Circle your answer.

Ray puts 18 pancakes on 3 plates. The first plate has 10 pancakes. The next plate has 3 pancakes. How many pancakes are on the last plate?

❶ Draw a picture to show the problem.

❷ Write a number sentence to solve the problem.

10 + _____ + _____ = 18

❸ Write your answer. _____

There are _____ pancakes on the last plate.

Directions: Read the problem. Solve the problem.

What shapes can you make with triangles?

1 Draw a shape using triangles.

2 Draw another shape using triangles.

3 Draw a third shape using triangles.

Directions: Color the things you have in your community.

51619–Conquering the Grades

© Shell Education

Directions: Follow the steps in this experiment to discover how to tell where things are.

What You Need

- items of different sizes or colors
- crayons or markers

What to Do

1 Work with a partner. Brainstorm words that can tell about where things are. Write the words.

_____

_____

_____

_____

_____

2 Take turns placing an object on a table. Say facts about its location. Repeat for each object.

3 Draw a picture to show where all the objects are.

Directions: Write the numbers 1–9 each on a slip of paper. Follow the directions below.

❶ Mix up the numbers. Then, write them in order counting forward.

_____

_ _ _ _ _ _ _ _ _ _ _ _ _ _ _ _ _ _ _ _

_____

❷ Mix up the numbers. Then, write them in order counting backward.

_____

_ _ _ _ _ _ _ _ _ _ _ _ _ _ _ _ _ _ _ _

_____

❸ Put the numbers back in the jar. Take out 2 numbers. Write the largest two-digit number you can make.

_____

_ _ _ _ _ _ _ _ _ _ _ _ _ _ _ _ _ _ _ _

_____

❹ Write the smallest two-digit number you can make.

_____

_ _ _ _ _ _ _ _ _ _ _ _ _ _ _ _ _ _ _ _

_____

Directions: Set up 10 water bottles like bowling pins. Take turns rolling a ball toward the bottles. Count how many are left standing. Write an X on that number on your scorecard. Reset the pins after each turn. The first player to mark off all the numbers wins.

Player 1: _____

0	1	2	3	4	5	6	7	8	9	10

Player 2: _____

0	1	2	3	4	5	6	7	8	9	10

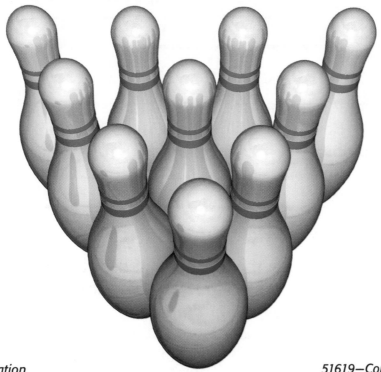

High-Frequency Words Activity

Read a book aloud to your child. Have him or her find any high-frequency words from page 144 in the book.

Writing Activity

Help your child revisit his or her writing from page 147. Have your child circle any high-frequency words that he or she used. If your child did not use any, help him or her add a sentence or revise one to include one of the words.

Problem-Solving Activity

Have your child draw pictures using squares. Then, have your child draw pictures using circles. Challenge your child to draw a picture using triangles, squares, and circles.

Social Studies Activity

Ask your child to name other places or landmarks in your community. Talk about what makes your community unique.

Critical-Thinking Activity

Have your child add the numbers 10–20 to his or her collection from page 154. Have your child repeat steps 1–4 on the page, using all 20 numbers.

Listening-and-Speaking Activity

Ask your child to compare the locations of different objects around your home. For example, *The apple is closer to me than the butter* or *The cup is on top of the table*.

Answer Key

There are many open-ended pages, problems, and writing prompts in this book. For those activities, the answers will vary. Answers are only given in this answer key if they are specific.

page 7

1. top
2. mop
3. pop
4. hop

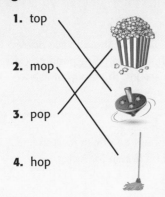

page 8

1. big
2. bib
3. bit
4. bin

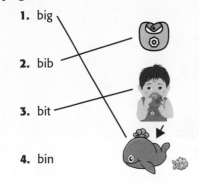

page 9

the — of
of — the
and ——— and
a — to
to — a

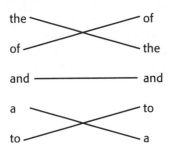

page 10

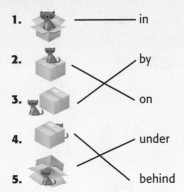

1. — in
2. — by
3. — on
4. — under
5. — behind

page 13

1. 3
2. 4
3. 5
4. 3
5. 5
6. 2

page 14

1. yes
2. no
3. no
4. yes

page 15

Picture should show seven bears, each wearing a hat.
There are 7 hats.

page 16

9; Student should have circled 9 flowers and drawn one leaf on each flower.

page 19

1. May
2. Madison
3. Morgan
4. Mary

Answer Key (cont.)

page 22

1. pop
2. jog
3. Mom
4. log

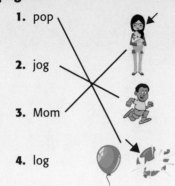

page 23

1. ten
2. vet
3. Ken
4. bed

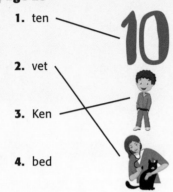

page 25

1. The
2. A
3. We
4. Can
5. I

page 26

All words except *lollipop* should be traced.

page 28

1. One string should be drawn on the kite.
2. Two legs should be drawn on the person.
3. All three blocks should be colored.
4. Four apples should be colored.
5. One more circle should be drawn for a total of five.
6. Six legs should be drawn on the ladybug.

page 29

1. pentagons
2. rectangles
3. circles
4. squares
5. Students should draw an oval on the left and a rectangle on the right.

page 30

5 is greater than 4; Student should have drawn lines to match each fish to a corresponding crab and drawn a circle around the group of fish to show the group is greater.

page 31

Rick; Two apples should be drawn for Ken and four apples should be drawn for Rick.

page 32

1.
2.
3.
4.

page 34

1. There should be an X over the circle.
2. There should be an X over the triangle.
3. There should be an X over the pentagon.
4. There should be an X over the pentagon.

page 37

1. hut
2. mug
3. tug
4. cup

page 38

1. top
2. tap
3. tip
4. tag

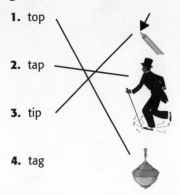

page 39
1. this
2. he
3. was
4. for
5. on

page 43
1. 10
2. 15
3. 12
4. 17
5. 14
6. 19

page 44
1. 8
2. 8
3. 9
4. 7
5. 9
6. 6

page 45

Eight flowers should be drawn.
Kenny has 8 flowers now.

page 46

5; Student should have drawn 5 blocks and counted them.

page 52

1. bat
2. bet
3. bit
4. bug

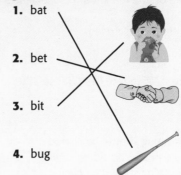

page 53

1. cot
2. cut
3. cat
4. can

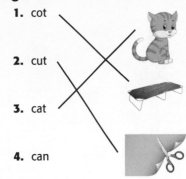

page 54
1. lrati aremesa
2. h with wtsklmt
3. yecslhya they
4. pmrsi haven pa
5. rsahw his hses

page 55
1. up
2. hot
3. big
4. go
5. top

page 58

1. The group on the left should be circled.
2. The box on the right should be circled.
3. There should be an X on the group on the left.
4. The bowl on the right should be circled.

page 59

1. 9
2. The machine on the left should be circled.
3. 20
4. All the fish should be circled.

page 60

A cube has 6 faces. A sphere has 0 faces. The cube should be circled.

page 61

1. 0 corners; nothing should be circled
2. 8 corners; 8 corners should be circled
3. 0 corners; nothing should be circled

page 64

Shape	Will it stack?	Will it slide?	Will it roll?
sphere	No	No	Yes
box	Yes	Yes	No
cylinder	Yes	Yes	Yes
cube	Yes	Yes	No

page 67

1. crib
2. fist
3. sing
4. lift

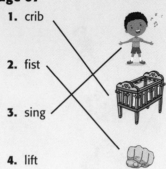

page 68

1. stop
2. lock
3. chop
4. crop

page 69

Student should have traced each word and written it twice on the lines.

page 70

1. b
2. e
3. g
4. h
5. i
6. r
7. t
8. y

page 71

All words should be traced.

page 73
1. 5
2. 7
3. 9
4. 6
5. 5
6. forward

page 74
1. The bathtub should be circled.
2. The milk carton should be circled.
3. The paper clip should be circled.
4. The mouse should be circled.
5. Example: a hat
6. Example: a swimming pool

page 75

7; Student should have counted on from 3.

Page 76

5; Student should have drawn 2 more bugs and counted on from 3.

page 83
1. C
2. A
3. A
4. B

page 84
1. It is (from) mom.
2. Do you like blue (or) red?
3. He has (one) truck.
4. I (had) a good day.
5. Sit (by) me.

page 85
1. boy
2. lamp
3. dog
4. girl
5. cat
6. desk

page 88
1. 5
2. 4
3. 5
4. 4
5. 5
6. 4

page 89
1. yes
2. 6
3. The triangle should be circled.
4. no
5. 0
6. Both squares and the rectangle should be colored.

page 90

Picture should show that Jess has 3 cats, Bob has 1 cat, and Leo has 4 cats.
Leo has the most cats.
Bob has the fewest cats.

page 91

Picture should show 4 slices of pizza. Three should be crossed out.
1 slice of pizza

page 92
1. day
2. week
3. month

page 94

Answer Key (cont.)

page 98
1. C
2. C
3. B
4. B

page 99
1. we
2. but
3. what
4. not

page 100
1. I like the pink cap.
2. Who will win?
3. The tent is wet.
4. Do not yell!
5. Who can mop?
6. Why did you go?
7. I love to read!
8. The pen is blue.

page 103
1. 15
2. 17
3. 18
4. All but three balls should be colored.
5. 14 bees (all but one) should be circled.
6. 13 sea stars (all but three) should be circled.

page 104
1. 1
2. 2
3. 1
4. 3
5. 4
6. 0

page 105
Student should have drawn 2 green frogs, 1 orange frog, and 5 red frogs for a total of 8 frogs.
$2 + 1 + 5 = 8$
There are 5 red frogs.

page 106
1. 4
2. There should be 4 groups: 4 tiny leaves in one group, 2 small leaves in a second group, 3 medium leaves in a third group, and 1 large leaf in the fourth group.
3. There should be a circle around the group with 1 large leaf.
4. There should be an X on the group with 4 tiny leaves.

page 107
1. Liberty Bell
2. American Flag
3. Statue of Liberty
4. bald eagle

page 109
1. chick
2. owlet
3. joey
4. pup
5. spiderling
6. piglet

page 113
1. A
2. B
3. A
4. B

page 115
1. ran
2. naps
3. fix
4. helps
5. grabs

page 116
All words should be traced.

page 118
1. Six circles should be drawn.
2. Two triangles should be drawn on the left, and more than two circles should be drawn on the right.
3. A set of circles that is more than 7 should be drawn.
4. 15 circles should be colored.

page 119
1. $4 + 1 = 5$
2. $2 + 2 = 4$
3. $2 - 2 = 0$
4. Student should have drawn two sets of one object each for a total of two objects.

page 120

Student should have drawn groups of 10 beads in 9 bags for a total of 90 beads.
9 bags

page 121
1. Possible answer: pencil; feather; stick
2. Possible answer: rock, big book, brick
3. Possible answer: airplane, truck; boat
4. Possible answer: seashell, penny; eraser

page 122

Clothes, water bottle, house, shoes and food should be colored. The game system, piano, and toy should be circled.

page 124
1. ant, mug, ruler, door
2. ant, ruler, mug, door

page 128
1. A
2. B
3. B
4. A

page 129
1. tudkehk**an**wtdeth
2. sr**use**qujezhpeib
3. wenbuxvd**each**nz
4. ainbn**said**kmipurw
5. dkipqug**there**ieoha

page 130
1. rake
2. rat
3. top
4. hit
5. bike

page 133
1. 11
2. 13
3. 14
4. 18
5. 20
6. 15

page 134
1. 4
2. 1
3. $2 - 1 = 1$
4. $3 - 3 = 0$
5. Five objects should be drawn, and one of them should be crossed out.
6. Four objects should be drawn, and two of them should be crossed out.

page 135

There should be two green dresses and two red dresses drawn, for a total of four dresses.
Kiki has 2 red dresses.

page 136

There should be three red balloons, three yellow balloons, and three blue balloons drawn, for a total of 9 balloons.
There are 3 blue balloons.

page 139
1. cat; cap; camp
2. mop; stop; nod
3. sit; bit; lip

page 143
1. C
2. A
3. C
4. B

page 144
1. **How** can we fix this?
2. **She** is my friend.
3. **Their** play was good.
4. **Which** one is bigger?
5. Can you **do** it?

page 145
1. dimes
2. ants
3. cones
4. games
5. lakes

page 146

All words should be traced.

page 148
1. 9
2. 8
3. 6
4. 11
5. 5
6. 16

page 149
1. 5
2. 4
3. 2
4. Five fish should be drawn.

page 150
1. Student should have drawn 10 pancakes on the first plate, 3 pancakes on the second plate, and 5 pancakes on the third plate.
2. $10 + 3 + 5 = 18$
3. There are 5 pancakes on the last plate.

page 151

Examples:

1.

2.

3.

Skills and Standards in This Book

Today's standards have created more consistency in how mathematics and English language arts are taught. In the past, states and school districts had their own standards for each grade level. However, what was taught at a specific grade in one location may have been taught at a different grade in another location. This made it difficult when students moved.

Today, many states and school districts have adopted new standards. This means that for the first time, there is greater consistency in what is being taught at each grade level, with the ultimate goal of getting students ready to be successful in college and in their careers.

Standards Features

The overall goal for the standards is to better prepare students for life. Today's standards have several key features:

- They describe what students should know and be able to do at each grade level.

- They are rigorous and dive deeply into the content.

- They require higher-level thinking and analysis.

- They require students to explain and justify answers.

- They are aimed at making sure students are prepared for college and/or their future careers.

Skills and Standards in This Book (cont.)

Unit Outline

This book is designed to help your child meet today's rigorous standards. This section describes the standards-based skills covered in each unit of study.

Unit 1

- Read simple, three-letter words.
- Practice reading and identifying high-frequency words.
- Use correct prepositions.
- Write a narrative about a picnic.
- Count up to 10.
- Draw pictures to solve word problems.
- Identify family members.
- Observe the weather over one day.

Unit 2

- Read simple, three-letter words.
- Practice reading and writing high-frequency words.
- Identify and use capital letters.
- Write an informative text about police officers.
- Count up to 10.
- Identify flat shapes.
- Compare numbers to determine which is larger.
- Identify goods and services that community workers provide.
- Push, pull, and twist objects.

Unit 3

- Read simple, three-letter words.
- Practice reading and writing high-frequency words.
- Determine how items are categorized.
- Write an opinion about a season.
- Count forward from a given number.
- Draw pictures to solve word problems.
- Identify what different community members have the authority to do.
- Use observable properties to identify a seed.

Unit 4

- Read simple, three-letter words.
- Practice reading and identifying high-frequency words.
- Identify the opposites of common words.
- Write a narrative about spending time with friends.
- Compare groups to determine which group has more objects.
- Count up to 20.
- Identify attributes of solid shapes.
- Make a time line of a day.
- Observe how different objects move in different ways.

Unit 5

- Read four-letter words with various blends.
- Practice reading and writing high-frequency words.
- Identify and use lowercase letters.
- Write an informative text about Earth's features.
- Count on to solve addition problems.
- Compare the sizes, weights, and capacities of objects.
- Identify natural features of Earth.
- Observe an animal.

Unit 6

- Read and answer questions about a narrative.
- Practice reading and writing high-frequency words.
- Identify nouns.
- Write an opinion about pets.
- Add within 10.

- Identify attributes of flat and solid shapes.
- Draw pictures to solve word problems.
- Use calendars to identify a day, week, and month.
- Observe the weather over five days.

Unit 7

- Read and answer questions about a piece of nonfiction text.
- Practice reading and writing high-frequency words.
- Use correct punctuation.
- Write a narrative about a birthday party.

- Count up to 20.
- Subtract within 10.
- Draw pictures to solve word problems.
- Identify American symbols.
- Observe how objects roll.

Unit 8

- Read and answer questions about a narrative.
- Practice reading and writing high-frequency words.
- Identify verbs.
- Write an informative text about ducks.
- Create sets that are more than, less than, or equal to a given number.

- Use equations to represent addition and subtraction problems.
- Use pictures to solve word problems.
- Identify whether objects are short, long, light, or heavy.
- Identify needs and wants.
- Sort objects by observable properties.

Unit 9

- Read and answer questions about a piece of nonfiction text.
- Practice reading and identifying high-frequency words.
- Use correct spelling of simple words.
- Write an opinion about desserts.
- Count up to 20.

- Use number sentences to show addition and subtraction problems.
- Subtract within 10.
- Draw pictures to solve word problems.
- Identify what community helpers do.
- Identify what humans need to survive.

Unit 10

- Read and answer questions about a narrative.
- Practice reading and writing high-frequency words.
- Identify and use plural nouns.
- Write an informative text about washing your hands.
- Compare numbers to determine which number is larger.

- Subtract within 10.
- Draw pictures to solve word problems.
- Compose simple shapes to form larger shapes.
- Identify community landmarks.
- Describe the relative locations of objects.

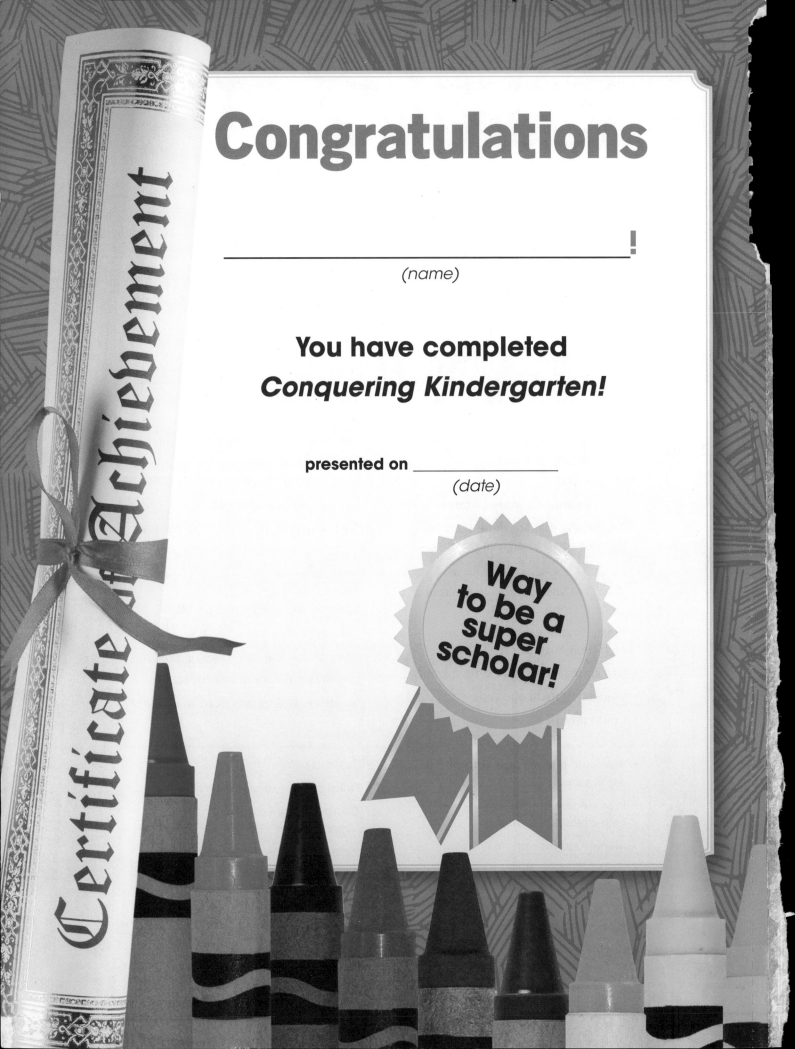